Speech(less) Presentation Basics

A Visual Guide

Mark Hartley Devlin

MARK HARTLEY DEVLIN

ISBN-13: 978-1492373780

ISBN-10: 1492373788

CONTENTS

Speech(less) Presentation Basics

A Visual Guide

PURPOSE

Speech(less) Presentation Basics: A Visual Guide was created for the sheer purpose of actually showing a presenter what they are "expected" to look like while making a presentation to an American audience. While teaching countless international college students how to effectively "make a speech," in my presentation classes, I decided to put some visuals together to serve an even broader audience. Presentation expectations in other countries are different than in the United States. This guide is not limited to students on their way to study in American universities but also useful for business people, travelers, and practically anyone interested in communicating with an American. Use this visual guide to get a heads up* of what is expected. Review it any time before you make a presentation.

I am sure you have been studying English a long time, so you know what you want to say. Now, you will be able to physically present your words in a manner that is pleasing and engaging to the American audience.

*heads up = warning

Whether watching a movie in the theater, watching a program on television, or listening to a fellow classmate make a presentation, the American audience is full of expectations. When you make a presentation to an American audience, particularly in the college classroom, they expect certain physical behavior from you. If you were not raised in the American environment, you might not know what this expected behavior would be.

This guide is for the purpose of bridging that expectation gap and showing you, visually, how you can engage your audience while presenting your information. Of course, these are just the basics. After you are comfortable with presenting in this manner, you will be able to add your own personal flair.

Presentation Basics

- Be prepared

- Know your topic

- Dress appropriately

- Smile

- Speak clearly

- Pronounce main words correctly using American English

- Use intonation in your voice when speaking – not monotone

- Try not to use filler sounds such as "uh" or "uhm"

- Make eye contact with your audience

- Keep your hands out of your pockets

Preparation – Your Appearance

Clean hair

Clear eyes*

Clean face

Smile

Clean shirt

Stand straight

Clean hands
and nails

*Not red (bloodshot) eyes

Be Inviting

Open arms

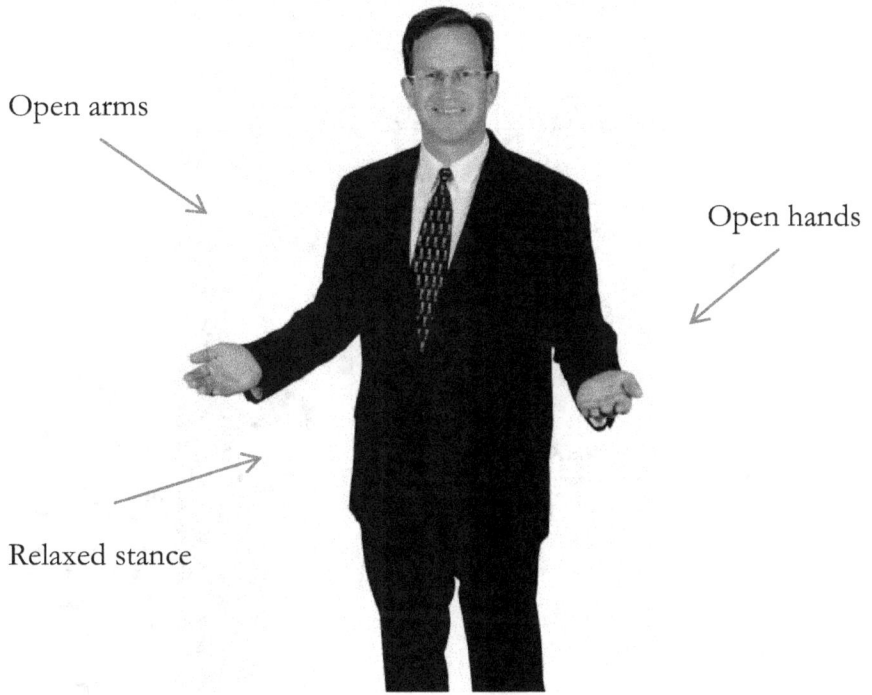

Open hands

Relaxed stance

Preparation – Other

Who is the audience?
English speakers?
How many people?
Age of the audience?

Do you have your materials?
Notes?
Slides?
Handouts?
Clicker/Laser Pointer?
Markers/Chalk?

Is the room ready?
Lights on or off?
Temperature?
Projector?
Computer?
Screen?
Microphone?
Whiteboard?
Lectern?
Air Conditioner/Heater noise?

Key to Symbols

O

X

American Style

Not American Style

See "Index to Visual Guide" on pages 32-35 for an
explanation of the photos

Greet Your Audience
(Begin your presentation)

O   X

Standing

O   X

Standing

O   X

Pointing to Screen

O   X

Pointing to Screen

O   X

Pointing to Screen

Advancing Slide Using Clicker

O   X

Distractions

Distractions

Writing on the Whiteboard

Reading from Paper

O   X

Reading from Paper

Reading from Paper

O   X

Reading from Paper

O   X

Reading from Paper

O   X

Reading from Paper

O   X

Reading from Notecards

O   X

Reading from Notecards

Answering Questions

O   X

Answering Questions

Answering Questions

O   X

Answering Difficult Questions

O   X

End Your Presentation
(Think About It)

Thanking the Audience

O   X

You Are Finished!

Index to Visual Guide

Title		Explanation	Page
Greet Your Audience	**O**	Open arms and hands Smile	6
	X	Arms behind back No smile	
Standing	**O**	Arms at side	7
	X	Arms behind back	
Standing	**O**	Open arms and hands Smile	8
	X	Hands in front / "Protection" No smile	
Pointing to Screen	**O**	Open arm / hand	9
	X	Arm crossing body	
Pointing to Screen	**O**	Open arm / hand	10
	X	Arm crossing body	
Pointing to Screen	**X**	Pointing behind / over shoulder Standing in front of screen	11
	X	Your back is to the audience Standing in front of screen	

Index to Visual Guide

Title		Explanation	Page
Advancing Slide Using Clicker	O	Open arm Face the audience	12
	X	Arm crossing body	
Distractions	X	Playing with marker	13
	X	Clicking pen	
Distractions	X	Playing with jewelry	14
	X	Playing with watch	
Writing on the Whiteboard	O	Left handed Writing is visible to the audience	15
	O	Right handed Writing is visible to the audience	
Reading from Paper	O	One hand / Arm's length Look at the audience	16
	X	Two hands Not relaxed / Too rigid	
Reading from Paper	O	One hand / Arm's length Look at the audience	17
	X	Two hands Reading from bottom of the page	

Index to Visual Guide

Title		Explanation	Page
Reading from Paper	**O**	One hand / Arm's length Look at the audience	18
	X	Two hands Paper too close to face	
Reading from Paper	**O**	One hand / Arm's length Look at the audience	19
	X	Two hands Is it heavy?	
Reading from Paper	**O**	One hand / Arm's length Look at the audience	20
	X	Writing on the back of the paper	
Reading from Paper	**O**	One hand / Arm's length Look at the audience	21
	X	Two hands Hiding from audience	
Reading from Notecards	**O**	One hand / Arm's length See the audience	22
	X	Too close to face	
Reading from Notecards	**O**	One hand / Arm's length Look at the audience	23
	X	Two hands Is it heavy?	

Index to Visual Guide

Title		Explanation	Page
Answering Questions	O	Could you repeat the question please?	24
	X	Are you angry?	
Answering Questions	O	Open arm / Open hand Smile	25
	X	Pointing with "middle" finger No smile	
Answering Questions	O	Open arm / Open hand Smile	26
	X	Pointing with one finger	
Answering Difficult Questions	O	"I'm thinking."	27
	X	"I don't know!"	
End Your Presentation	O	Relaxed Smile	28
	O	Gesture for audience to think about your information	
Thanking the Audience	O	Open arms and hands Smile	29
	X	"Bowing" is not expected	

Speech(less) Quick Review

Speech(less) Quick Review

Note to Instructors

- Make a copy of "Speech(less) Quick Review."
- Give students feedback by circling the X or the O during their presentation.
- Give the students a copy of their feedback.

ABOUT THE AUTHOR

Mark Hartley Devlin, MA TESOL, BA Business, teaches English as a second language to international college students in San Diego, California. Born and raised in the United States of America, he has a good understanding of what Americans expect.

www.ingramcontent.com/pod-product-compliance
Lightning Source LLC
Chambersburg PA
CBHW072251310526
45795CB00011B/941